CECIL BEATON

CECIL BEATON

Phillipe Garner

COLLINS

CECIL BEATON

by Philippe Garner

Cecil Beaton in Austria, 1937

Beaton's was a unique talent, more precisely a unique combination of talents, which made him a singularly gifted chronicler of over half a century of fashions, styles, people and places. Through six decades, from his earliest, precocious tentatives in the twenties until thwarted by ill health in the seventies, he worked with limitless energy and demonstrated an increasingly wide range of skills, earning international respect as photographer, diarist and designer.

He is perhaps best known to the public as the most distinguished of 'royal photographers' and as creator of the memorable settings and costumes for the 1964 film version of *My Fair Lady*. However, he was also highly respected as an author and critic, an exhibition designer, an artist capable of the most astute and incisive graphic as well as literary sketches, a gifted decorator, a fine host and a sparkling conversationalist.

Beaton was a dandy and an aesthete and his was a seemingly magical touch. A man of considerable personal elegance and grace, Beaton would always adopt a relaxed and unflurried pose, yet he had an enormous capacity for hard work, whilst producing results which preserved the illusion of ease and facility. His friend, American author Truman Capote observed in his introduction to *The Best of Beaton* that, 'Though he is apparently always under the pressure of a disheartening schedule, one would never suppose he wasn't a gentleman of almost tropical leisure.' Behind the leisured façade was a highly developed, albeit often precious, aesthetic sensibility and a single-minded determination to make his mark on the twentieth century.

Beaton was driven by ambition. This character trait fuelled him with a tremendous appetite for work but earned him a less enviable reputation in certain eyes for his ruthlessness in striving towards his goals. He was a snob, a prerequisite surely of the sophisticated aesthete, but not always in the generally accepted, derogatory sense of social exclusivity. There is no denying the arrogant snobbery of Beaton's early years, including his time at university at Cambridge and, indeed, in these years his snobbery and ambition were inextricably interwoven driving forces. A more compassionate side to his character was to emerge however, and, through the veil of his fascination with an elitist world of the talented, the titled, the wealthy, and the beautiful, his photographs, as indeed his sketches and writings, are filled with a very human sensitivity towards his subjects. If his snobbery persisted, it was in a very positive sense, in his eternal pursuit of standards of excellence.

Beaton's deceptive lightness of touch, his ability to conjure up a delicate and fragile world of sophisticated artifice and seductiveness were skills which made him a masterful stage and film designer, and which, of course, served him in great stead as a fashion and portrait photographer. It has been said of Beaton, however, that his greatest creation was himself, his carefully constructed image of a charmed life. Certainly there is much illusionism in the Beaton style and the accusations of artifice levelled at his photography by critics whose preference is for the supposedly 'pure' applications of the medium are not without some justification. Artifice is a major ingredient of Beaton's photographic work. But human sensitivity is there also in sufficient strength for his images to escape the barrenness of purely stylistic exercises. In entering Beaton's photographic world one is obliged to shelve one's own vision of the world in order to taste fully the flavour of *his* reality, of the world seen through his remarkable eyes, both experienced and expressed through his equally remarkable life and ultimately captured through his lens.

Beaton's first stirrings of interest in photographic images were experienced at the age of three. He tells of the occasion when, on his mother's bed, as she read her post, he was captivated by a postcard portrait of actress Lily Elsie. The infant Beaton was to become increasingly fascinated by the postcard portraits of the great theatre beauties of the Edwardian era, by Gabrielle Ray, Gladys Cooper, his beloved Lily Elsie and others of their generation. He collected these cards and in his *My Fair Lady* designs (often inspired from the photographic studies published in *The Play Pictorial*) paid full homage to this first shaping influence on his aesthetic. The photographic world with which the young Beaton was most familiar was the somewhat formalized and stilted world of the society and theatrical portrait studios of the twenties, and he loved the glamour and the flattery which were their stock in trade. The painted backdrops, soft focus effects and tricks of retouching were imitated and developed by the young Beaton and, writing in 1975 in *The Magic Image* of the portrait studios of the early decades of this century, he showed an obvious nostalgic fondness for the work of Alice Hughes, Rita Martin, Lallie Charles and Dorothy Wilding and the studios of Elliott & Fry or Messrs Foulsham & Bamfield and their rivals, for the most part clustered around fashionable Bond Street in London's Mayfair.

The predominant style of photography enjoying favour in the twenties, and to which Beaton was inevitably attracted, was Pictorialism. By the twenties the ideals of two movements concerned to establish photography as a fine art, the British Linked Ring and Alfred Stieglitz's American Photo-Secessionists, had degenerated into an uninspired and predictable artiness in a Salon style canonized in England in the annual exhibitions of the Royal Photographic Society and the pages of *Photograms of the Year*. Beaton's aspiration was to see his work hung in the Society's Salon and the appearance of his 1922 portrait 'Boy Lebas' (page 13) in *Photograms of the Year* was amongst his first successes in seeing his work published.

The greatest single influence on Beaton's early work, however, was the fashion photographer and portraitist Baron de Meyer, whose distinctive images were seen and enjoyed by Beaton in the pages of *Vogue*. Beaton found lyrical phrases to describe the features of de Meyer's work, which he admired and emulated. He called de Meyer 'the Debussy of the camera' and could just as easily have been describing his own early work when he wrote: 'He used artificial light to make an aurora borealis. He discovered a soft focus yet pin-point sharp lens which gave the required extra sparkle to shiny surfaces . . . He invented a new universe; a high-key world of water sparkling with sunshine, or moonlight and candlelight . . . of tissues and gauzes, of pearly lustre and dazzling sundrops.'

Beaton was entranced by the sparkling world of fashion and high society which de Meyer's tricks of light evoked so perfectly and he absorbed de Meyer's techniques in the development of his own style, acknowledging this debt by signing his photographs in exactly the same style of lettering as used by de Meyer. Beaton also acknowledged the influence in his early years of the American photographer, Edward Steichen, though this is a less discernible source. The other notable photographer to influence Beaton was the aristocratic George Hoyningen-Huené. Recalling their trip to North Africa together in 1931, Beaton wrote in *The Wandering Years*: 'Following in Huené's steps, I started to make, out of the life around me, pictures that attempted to be interesting as compositions, to bring a point of view to the subject and, if possible, to make a comment. To George my thanks are

In entering Beaton's photographic world, one is obliged to shelve one's own vision of the world in order to taste fully the flavour of his reality . . .

proferred for adding this additional pleasure to travel and an extra facet to my photographic career.'

After this date and his evidently instructive time spent with Huené, it becomes difficult to trace the influence of other photographers in Beaton's work, for his independent spirit was to make itself increasingly marked. He drew ideas from numerous sources but was more likely to adapt a painterly conceit to the photographic idiom than lean on the work of other practitioners in the same medium. In fact, through the thirties, Beaton was to explore the imagery of surrealism and fashionable neo-romantic styles within still life, fashion and portrait photography and forged lasting links with figures in the worlds of art, decoration, film and letters, whose ideas, shared with and, as likely, nurtured by the catalystic Beaton, were translated into photographic imagery.

Beaton's energy has always maintained its momentum on a constant diet of ideas exchanged with friends, on things observed, absorbed, learned from other equally intuitive spirits. Beaton developed with the times, evolved his style in keeping with whilst never slave to changing fashions, and, after a brief period from the late fifties into the early sixties when he was perhaps regarded as unfashionable, he surfaced with a renewed photographic zest, inspired by young friends, painters, rock stars and a new generation of trend-setters to find a fresh approach to photography.

After a brief period ... when he was perhaps regarded as unfashionable, he surfaced with a renewed photographic zest, inspired by young friends, painters, rock stars and a new generation of trend-setters to find a fresh approach to photography.

The fashionable world has always been Beaton's natural habitat, the backdrop to his own colourful life-style and to his creativity. Within this world Beaton shone in many roles—master of the pen, the artist's pencil, master of the aesthete and arbiter's gesture and, most conspicuously, of the camera. Photography provided him with a profession through which he could flirt with the allied worlds of society, the arts and fashion as well as with the means of creating his own highly personalized document of these intriguing worlds. Photography, as a truly amateur passion, also gave him the opportunity to create a private, more intimate document of his own travels through life, as he compiled over the years a remarkable series of 'snapshot' albums in which contact-printed photo sequences tell the story of his life and provide a visual complement to his diaries (pages 10 and 11).

Beaton's interest in photography went still further. He had a boundless appetite for images as can be well appreciated from the variety and contrasts to be found within the scrapbooks which he pasted up over the years, notably in his later years, in which original prints by Julia Margaret Cameron or de Meyer shared place with magazine tear-sheets of photographs by Richard Avedon or Irving Penn.

Unlike so many photographers who work within a very limited stylistic range and often to restricting, self-imposed rules, Beaton always faced the medium with open-mindedness, adapting his approach to the circumstances but always showing an instinctive sympathy with the potentials of the medium. His lack of dogmatism made him one of the few active photographers to also prove himself as a photo-historian and critic. He had a very broad knowledge of both nineteenth and twentieth century photography and could appreciate the work of photographers as diverse as Nadar, Emerson, Weston and Penn.

His first publication on the history of photography was his *British Photographers,* of 1944. His last and most impressive contribution to the study of the history of photography was the aptly titled *The Magic Image,* published in 1975. This excellent work, in which Beaton's pithy and often biting turns of phrase

continued on page 57

THE
PHOTOGRAPHS

Rex Whistler, early 1920s

serse   Ballet — Cecil & Serge — Venice v. 1933

10

alexandre wollhoff Haas, Renin-Chips

Pages from one of Beaton's
snapshot albums, Venice, 1933

11

Boy Lebas, Cambridge, 1922

Marlene Dietrich, America, 1935

Marlene Dietrich, Salzburg, 1930

Greta Garbo, Plaza Hotel, New York, 1946

Gary Cooper, Hollywood, 1931

Orson Welles, 1930s

Marilyn Monroe, New York, 1956

Victor Kraft, 1930s

Margot Fonteyn, New York, 1967

Jean Cocteau, Toulon, 1945

Charles Henry Ford, 1930s

24

Salvador Dali and his wife, Gala, 1936

Gertrude Stein, 1945

Colette, Paris, 1953

Aldous Huxley, 1936

Carol Reed, 1940

Renée, a Dior model, Paris, 1955

Wartime fashion, London, September 1941

Girl in opera coat, London, 1928

Marian Moorehouse, New York, 1930

Charles James evening dresses, New York, 1948

Lady Oxford, London, 1927

Countess of Jersey, Osterley, 1935

Mary Taylor, 1930s

Portrait study, date unknown

Daisy Fellowes, Venice, 1951

Queen Elizabeth,
Buckingham Palace, 1939

The Duchess of Windsor, Candé, France, 1937

Ouled Nails, Morocco, 1937

Spain, 1960

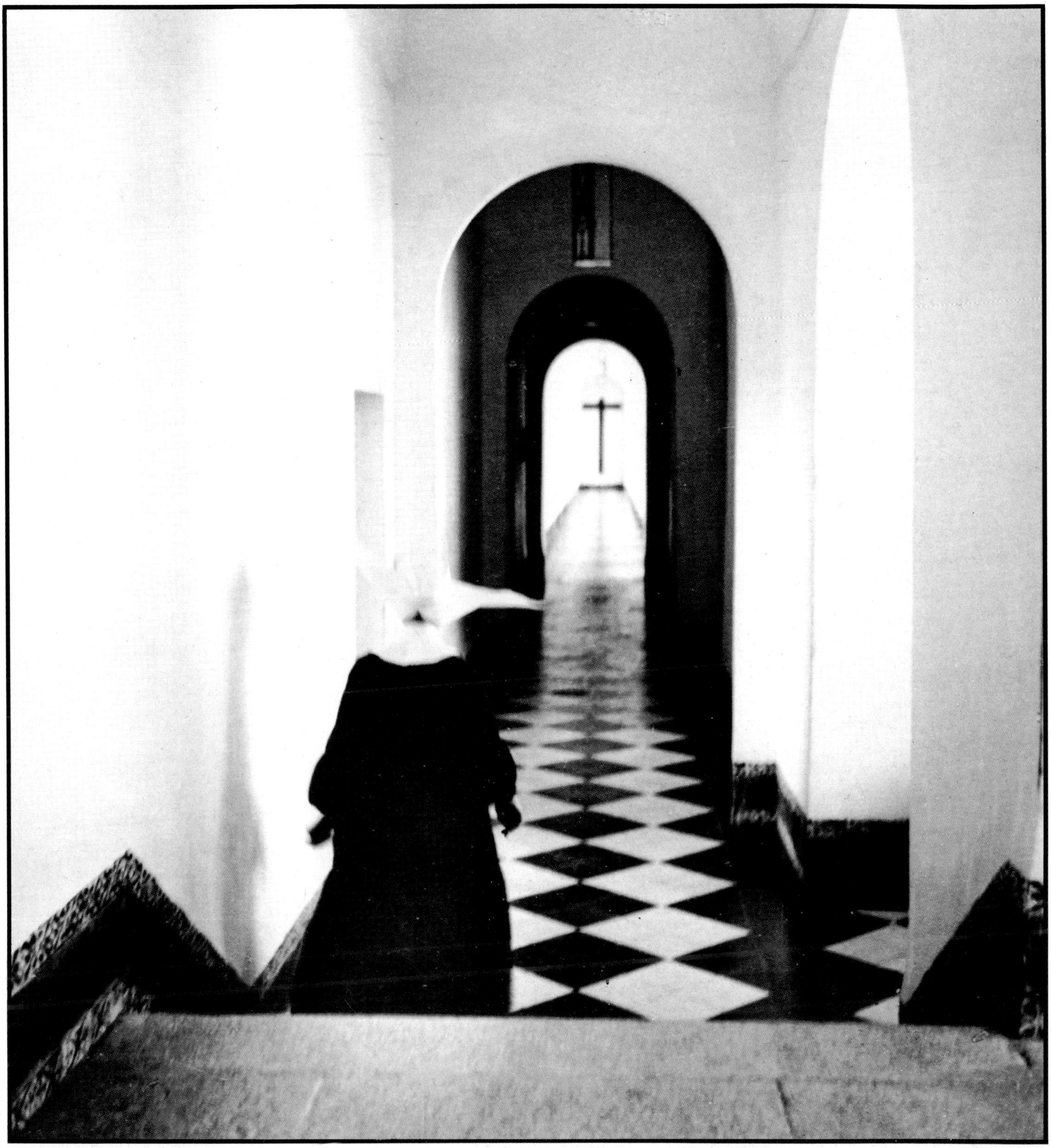

New York, 1937

New York, 1937

Chinese Military Police, 1945

War wreckage, Sidi Rezegh, Libya, 1942

Bombed fire station, Tobruck, 1942

Sandstorm in the Libyan desert, 1942

Interior of Charles de Bestegui's home, 1941

Keith Richard, Morocco, 1967

David Hockney, 1969

Viva, New York, November, 1969

Andy Warhol and entourage, New York, April 1969

Marilyn Monroe,
New York, 1956

David Warner, 1965 or 1966

Girl reading, *circa* 1950

Jean Shrimpton, London, 1966

Katherine Hepburn, 1955

continued from page 6

analysed the evolution of the medium from its very beginnings to the 1970s, was the fruit of a lifetime's experience and reflections. It shows a unique breadth of understanding of the infinite potential of photography.

Cecil Beaton's earliest recollections of the impact of photographic images were his childhood souvenirs of musical comedy postcards, but his first attempts at photography came some years later when, aged eleven, he acquired his first camera, a No. 3A folding Kodak. Inspired by and helped by his sisters' nurse, Alice Collard, herself a keen amateur whose snapshots of the family had thrilled the young Beaton, he turned his hand to making romantic, glamorized portraits of his young sisters and of his mother. He learned to develop and to print by a costly process of trial and error. He experimented with lighting, using multiple light sources and reflecting mirrors to achieve the theatrical haloes and sparkles which he sought. Considerable ingenuity transformed sheets, carpets and scraps into exotic Spanish or medieval costumes and he devised clever printing techniques, such as the placing of a sheet of glass between negative and paper during exposure or the use of a soft filter during half the exposure. In his passion for shimmering effects and reflective surface, Beaton used mirrors, crumpled tin foil, cellophane and American cloth and he readily admitted that his sitters' personalities became subordinate to the play of light and decorative effect.

He readily admitted that his sitters' personalities became subordinate to the play of light and decorative effect.

Throughout his school years at Harrow and subsequently at university at Cambridge, Beaton continued to experiment with his photography, using the medium to capture what appear as somewhat camp and contrived moments from elaborate amateur theatricals or country idylls. His sisters were ever willing to play out various roles and at Cambridge he met a generation of bright young things whose air of fragile youth was immortalized through the Beaton lens. His portrait of the young Rex Whistler in a country setting is an exquisite souvenir of those heady days (page 9). As early as 1924, Beaton found his way into the pages of *Vogue* with the publication of his study 'The Duchess of Malfi', in reality a transvestite portrait of his friend George Rylands.

Leaving Cambridge, without taking his degree exams and under pressure from his father, Beaton took up an office employment which was very much against his natural inclinations and his own time was devoted to attracting willing society figures and celebrities as sitters, working towards building up a portfolio adequate for ultimate exhibition in a London West End gallery. Encouraged by a preliminary trickle of portrait commissions, Beaton left his employer in September 1926 to launch himself professionally as a photographer.

Working from the family home in London's Sussex Gardens, Beaton attracted a flurry of interest through the novelty and inventiveness of his style of portraiture. Amongst the most memorable portraits from these early professional years were his studies of William Walton the composer, in profile against an aggressively angular painted geometric backdrop (page 8); his 1927 portrait of Lady Oxford, against a bold art deco painted backdrop (page 35); his tender 1926 portrait of the young Daphne du Maurier; and his graphically striking and expressive study of the young poetess Nancy Cunard, her arms weighed down with barbaric bracelets, against a giant polka-dot backcloth (page 12).

Beaton's originality was already outweighing the influence of his early heroes, and it was this originality which attracted the interest and patronage of an eccentric but most influential, aristocratic and artistic family, the Sitwells. Sacheverell and his wife Georgia, Osbert and, above all, Edith became regular sitters and most willing participants in Beaton's fanciful tableaux. The Sitwells were at the forefront of Britain's artistic avant-garde and their support confirmed Beaton's position as the most fashionable and exciting young portraitist. Beaton was to capture perfectly, through numerous sittings, the grandiose eccentricity of this family, notably of Edith (page 58), whose features he recorded into old age. The fruits of about two years of professional activity were eventually shown in a Bond Street exhibition where Beaton's distinctive portraits of beauties, celebrities and society figures attracted a most favourable press. Success seemed assured.

Amongst those whose attentions were drawn to Beaton's portraits was Mrs Edna Chase, editor of American *Vogue,* who, on a visit to London, threw out an invitation of work, should Beaton find himself in the United States. Late in 1929 Beaton was on his way to New York. Awaiting him was a whole new social register and it was not long before New York's society ladies, led by Mrs Harrison Williams, were finding their way to Beaton's improvised studio in the Ambassador Hotel. Decorator and socialite Elsie de Wolfe staged an exhibition of Beaton's photographs, shown alongside his drawings and watercolours. The greatest success of the trip, however, was the fulfilment of Mrs Edna Chase's promise. Beaton was introduced to Mr Condé Nast and signed a contract to take photographs for *Vogue,* for what was then a princely salary.

From this trip dates an elegant series of fashion studies for *Vogue,* taken in Condé Nast's apartment with the stunning Miss Marian Moorehouse (page 32) and Lee Miller as models. The portrait photographer had added a new string to his bow as fashion photographer and sailed back to England flushed with success. On his return he put together and published his first book, *The Book of Beauty,* in 1930, an anthology of photographs, sketches and words which serves as a résumé of the first phase of his career. It included portraits of eminent sitters on both sides of the Atlantic, among them Lillian Gish, Alice White, Marion Davies, Norma Shearer, Edith Sitwell, Tallulah Bankhead, Lily Elsie, Lady Diana Cooper and the Marquise de Casa Maury.

After London and New York, Beaton's next conquest was Hollywood where he devised a host of new ideas to photograph cinema stars. Ever inventive, he worked in artificial light but also exploited the strong sunlight of California with its graphic patterns of shadows to produce a striking portfolio of portraits which escaped the usual stereotyped formulae. He produced a marvellous series of studies of the young and handsome Gary Cooper, in one memorable shot dwarfed by the giant doors of the studio (page 17). He photographed the rugged Johnny Weissmuller as Tarzan, Dolores del Rio as a South Seas beauty, Buster Keaton, Carole Lombard, John Wayne and numerous others. Beaton was at home and his talent shone in the city which manufactured myths.

The thirties were busy years for Beaton. He travelled far and wide taking in such diverse locations as North Africa and Spain, Russia, Palm Beach and Mexico, and everywhere society's doors were flung open for this charming, talented and entertaining Englishman. The considerable body of work compiled by Beaton during this decade covers every range of his photographic spectrum—the portraits of an ever wider cast of prominent figures from the worlds of entertainment and the arts and from high society, a flow of increasingly professional fashion work and the

Edith Sitwell, Renishaw, 1927

ever fascinating images which documented the unfolding of his own life and his endless travels.

From the thirties date such imaginative portraits as that of Charles Henry Ford, the young surrealist poet, a black silhouette covered with surgical rubber gloves and his features concealed by giant hands (page 24); Salvador Dali with his wife weaving a fencing mask (page 25); the fine series of portraits of the inimitable Jean Cocteau, his exquisite dandyism and perversity so perfectly understood and expressed by the photographer (page 23); and the simple but so effective glimpse of Aldous Huxley behind a torn cloth (page 28). Beaton put together baroque props to create surreal settings; he used the simplest of tricks, torn paper, to the maximum effect. Yet he was equally capable of making a stunning portrait with no props at all, using just his lights and his persuasive coaxings to reveal his sitters in characteristic and usually flattering poses. His two portraits of Marlene Dietrich demonstrate his range, from the uncluttered and sensitive study made in her hotel suite in Salzburg in 1930 (page 15), to the ravishing, highly stylized and mannered profile study of 1935 (pages 14–15). Amongst his conquests he could also list Colette (page 26), Picasso, Christian Bérard, Marie Laure de Noailles, Danilova, Laurence Olivier, Serge Lifar and countless other bright lights. He continued, meanwhile, his document of English society and aristocratic life, producing such evocative images as his portrait of Lady Jersey in Robert Adam's colonnade at Osterley (page 34).

In his fashion work for *Vogue,* Beaton devised witty and stylish settings appropriate to the fashions which he was documenting. Stark, dramatic sets for boldly cut clothes by Schiaparelli or Charles James; whimsical backdrops for romantic evening dresses; and frequently he would create scenarios as if the fashion shot were just one still in a film sequence with a story line left to the imagination.

Of his travel photographs from the thirties the most interesting essay was surely his 1937 series on New York, many of which were published in 1938 in his *Portrait of New York*. Seemingly spontaneous snapshots, these images of New York are confident and well-balanced compositions, telling images in which an unusual viewpoint or unexpected subject jolts the viewer into a new awareness of a familiar city (pages 42 and 43). Also in 1937 Beaton made a series of photographic studies in the *quartiers réservés* of Morocco and amongst these are such fine photographs as his interior scene with two figures which is a truly painterly composition with the qualities of space and perspective of an interior by Vermeer (page 40).

In the busy year of 1937 Beaton received an important commission, first to take a series of portraits of Mrs Wallis Simpson (page 39) to promote a rather more appealing image than that with which the British public was so far familiar and, soon after, he was asked to officiate as photographer at her marriage to the Duke of Windsor. Two years later, and despite his associations with the exiled Duke and Duchess of Windsor, Beaton was summoned to Buckingham Palace to take portraits of the Queen. After the upheavals of the abdication, the public image of the royal family was at a low ebb, but if any one series of photographs must be given credit for revitalizing this image it is this magnificent, grand and romantic sequence of portraits of the Queen, posed in tiara and full-skirted gowns in the grand interiors and in the gardens of the Palace (page 38). This royal accolade provided Beaton with an impressive finale to a most successful decade.

The outbreak of war in 1939 was to mark the beginning of a new phase in his

Despite his associations with the exiled Duke and Duchess of Windsor, Beaton was summoned to Buckingham Palace to take portraits of the Queen.

career. Abandoning the essentially frivolous aspects of so much of his work, he devoted himself to his duties as official war photographer for the Ministry of Information. These duties involved him in assignments to record the bomb damage inflicted on London (page 30) and the activities of the R.A.F. at their bases throughout England, and subsequently took him on postings, first to North Africa, where he covered the war in the desert, and then to the Far East.

Beaton's coverage of these varied aspects of the war had been, until the 1974 major exhibition organized by the Imperial War Museum, a less well-known aspect of his work, but his war photographs provide a valuable insight into his *modus operandi*. For here is subject matter which is diametrically opposed, surely, to that to which Beaton would naturally have been attracted. He managed, nonetheless, through pure photographic instinct and an exceptionally keen and sensitive eye to take photographs which captured the mood of the British at war and which transformed the debris of war into the most memorable of images. Certain of his war photographs are justly celebrated, such as his injured child in a hospital bed (page 60), a photograph published on the cover of *Life* magazine and credited with having swayed American opinion into entering the war; his elegant ragged abstractions composed from the ruined remnants of tanks in the desert (page 45) or of a collapsed, bombed-out building in Tobruk (page 46); his frightening sandstorm, a soldier clutching his way towards the safety of his tent (page 47). But his war work extends to many thousands of negatives, from reflective still-life subjects to fleeting snapshots, an unlikely body of work yet one stamped with the inimitable mark of his acutely observant and sophisticated eye.

Returning to civilian life, Beaton took up the threads of his career, travelling, photographing, designing. The immediate postwar years saw some of his very best fashion work and it is tempting to single out his shimmering, Watteau-like study of 1948, a complex composition with eight models in evening dresses by Charles James, as a high point of the genre (page 33). Beaton's theatrical fashion style was becoming outdated, however, and new talents, notably Richard Avedon and Irving Penn, were the rising stars in this field. By the mid-fifties Beaton's contract with *Vogue* was terminated.

In his portraiture Beaton was becoming more interested in capturing the vulnerability and reality of his sitters than in perpetually flattering them. Writing in the early fifties, he rejected his pre-war frivolities, having had '. . . enough of taking fashions on young models who survive just as long as their faces show no signs of character, or of elderly but rich harpies appearing as if butter would not melt in their terrible mouths'.

James Danziger, in the essay introducing his 1980 anthology of Beaton's work, wrote that, 'By 1957 the typical Beaton subject was no longer a smart young thing seen in all his or her finery, but a study of the effects of age on beauty, or the changes wrought by experience on the faces of the personalities of a generation.' The quotation calls to mind Beaton's powerful portraits of the ageing Colette (page 26), the wizened Cocteau, or his portraits of Monroe, appearing unexpectedly exposed and pathetic (page 52).

During these years and into the sixties much of Beaton's energy was taken up in work for stage and screen, with his designs for *Gigi* and *My Fair Lady* in particular winning him wide and well-deserved acclaim. The sixties meanwhile witnessed a major upheaval in British cultural life and Beaton found much to inspire him in the

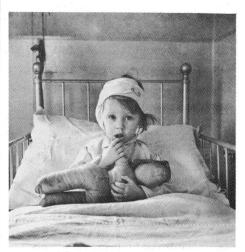

Eileen Dunne, aged 3, in hospital, 1940. The photograph was published on the cover of *Life* and is credited with having swayed American opinion about entering World War II.

energetic and youthful generation with which he eagerly associated. The Rolling Stones (page 49), David Hockney (page 49), Peter Blake, David Bailey, Rudolph Nureyev and Andy Warhol and his entourage (page 50) are a few amongst the many new friends and sitters who gave a quite fresh character to this latter phase of Beaton's photographic activity. His portraits from this period tend to be more straightforward, stark and direct than those associated with former decades.

But history was meanwhile catching up with Beaton and he was made increasingly aware of his role, less as a still-fashionable photographer than as a grand old man of British photography, perhaps, alongside Bill Brandt, the most highly regarded. A major retrospective exhibition of his work staged in 1968 at the National Portrait Gallery in London followed in 1974 by the Imperial War Museum exhibition of his war work made him ironically aware that he had become a legend and that many people were speaking of him in the past tense. A paralysing stroke suffered in 1974 marked the effective end of a distinguished career as a photographer, though his 1979 coverage of the Paris autumn collections for French *Vogue* demonstrated his gritty determination not to give up. In 1977 he sold to Sotheby's, the London art auctioneers, almost his entire archive of prints and negatives and he found both amusement and satisfaction in observing the marketing at increasingly high prices of the prints that were the relics of this distinguished career. Beaton died in his bed in the early morning of 18 January 1980.

The finest commentator on Beaton's photographs is surely Beaton himself and the numerous illustrated books which he published over the decades—a potpourri of words, sketches and photographs—provide an invaluable insight into the sensibility which drove him to take so many of these photographs. Beaton's words, epigramatic, witty and expressive, give an added dimension to his images. Typical are the phrases which he coined to describe one of his earliest celebrity sitters, Nancy Cunard, whose portrait was published in his very first book, *The Book of Beauty,* in 1930 (page 12). 'Her appearance', he wrote, 'is very Egyptian, with Nefertiti's long upper lip and slightly pointing mouth, which she paints like a crimson scar across her face. Her hair is metal blonde, her cheek bones pronounced, her nose a little blunt and finely sensitive, her movements rhythmical. She resembles a robot woman in a German film . . .'

Beaton's next book was a more extensive anthology of experiences, published in 1937 under the title *Cecil Beaton's Scrapbook.* Snapshots from his travels vie for space with fashion studies and posed portraits, and the accompanying text reveals his delight in visual stimulation, in the savouring of beauty. He describes one of his favourite models, Mary Taylor (page 36), as having '. . . about her the suggestion of a Balinese dancer, with her fastidious bud-like hands, preening movements of her head and careful walk. The arched eyebrows, lowered lids, recoiling nostrils, combined with her strange whiteness and stem-like neck, create an effect of exotic rarity. She is like an Oriental idol. . . .'

More titles appeared over the years, amongst these most notably his *Portrait of New York* in 1938, *The Glass of Fashion* in 1954, *The Face of the World* in 1957, the various volumes of his diaries and, in 1968, his final anthology *The Best of Beaton.* Beaton's descriptive powers, powers of observation which make his photographs as rich as his words, are well exemplified in his evocation of Monroe's elusive charm in the text which accompanied his 1956 portraits of the actress (page 19), published in the following year in *The Face of the World.* 'She is,' he wrote, 'as spectacular as

Technical note

Beaton's first camera was a No. 3A folding pocket Kodak. His earliest work is characterized by often extensive retouching both on the negative and on the print, though in later years he was less inclined to retouch his images. It was at the insistence of Condé Nast that he started to work on larger format plate cameras, his first being a 10×8 inch (25×20cm) camera with 12 inch (300mm) f/6.3 Kodak Commercial Ektar lens and he favoured this format for studio work through the thirties, forties and into the fifties, using smaller formats for his work in the field. In later years he favoured the $2\frac{1}{4} \times 2\frac{1}{4}$ inch (6×6cm) format of the Rolleiflex which he first used extensively during the war. Beaton made his own prints in the early years as amateur and professional, but subsequently entrusted the printing of his work to others, always favouring warm tones and, in later years, stipple-textured papers.

Marilyn Monroe, Beaton wrote, 'is as spectacular as the silvery shower of a Vesuvius fountain . . . In her presence, you are startled, then disarmed, by her lack of inhibition.'

the silvery shower of a Vesuvius fountain . . . Transfigured by the garish marvels of technicolour and cinemascope, she walks like an undulating basilisk . . . Her voice, of a loin-stroking affection, has the sensuality of silk or velvet . . . In her presence, you are startled, then disarmed, by her lack of inhibition. What might at first seem like exhibitionism is yet counterbalanced by a wistful incertitude beneath the surface.' All is captured by Beaton in the click of his shutter.

Truman Capote, introducing *The Best of Beaton,* pays homage to the photographer's eye and his words provide a fine epitaph to a remarkable talent. 'His visual intelligence,' he wrote, 'is genius . . . To listen to Beaton describe in strictly visual terms a person or room or landscape is to hear a recitation that can be hilarious or brutal or very beautiful but will always certainly be brilliant. And that, the unusual visual intelligence infiltrating his pictures . . . is what makes Beaton's work unusually separate; the preservative for which our next-century historians will be even more grateful than we are now.'

Chronology

1904
Born 14 January in London.

1915
Given first camera, age eleven.

1917
Started school at Harrow, age thirteen.

1922
Arrives at Cambridge University, 4 October.

1924
Beaton's study 'Duchess of Malfi' published in *Vogue.*

1926
Leaves his employment and launches himself professionally as photographer.

1929
First trip to New York, leading to work for Condé Nast.

1931
First trip to Hollywood and other travels including visit to North Africa with George Hoyningen-Huené.

1936
Exhibition of paintings and stage designs, Redfern Gallery, London.

1937
Trip to New York and various other travels.
Portraits of the Duke and Duchess of Windsor.

1939
First royal portrait commission.

1940
Assigned to Ministry of Information. Works in London.

1941
Assigned to cover R.A.F. activities throughout U.K.

1942
Posted to Cairo for Ministry of Information.

1943-4
Travels in Far East for Ministry of Information.

1956
First work for *Harper's Bazaar,* New York.

1957
Sets and costumes for *Gigi* win Beaton's first Oscar.

1964
My Fair Lady and Beaton's set and costume designs win his second Oscar.

1968
National Portrait Gallery retrospective exhibition.

1972
Receives knighthood.

1974
Imperial War Museum Exhibition of War Photographs.
Suffers stroke in July.

1977
Sale of his photographic archive to Sotheby's.

1979
Covers Paris fashion collections for French *Vogue.*

1980
Died 18 January, age seventy six.

Bibliography

The Book of Beauty, London, 1930.
Cecil Beaton's Scrapbook, London, 1937.
Portrait of New York, London, 1938.
My Royal Past, London 1939.
History Under Fire, with James Pope
    Hennessy, London, 1941.
Time Exposure, with Peter Quennell,
    London, 1941.
Air of Glory: A Wartime Scrapbook,
    London, 1941.
Winged Squadrons, London, 1942.
Near East, London, 1943.
British Photographers, London, 1944.
Far East, London, 1945.
India, Bombay, 1945.
An Indian Album, London, 1945/6.
Chinese Album, London, 1945/6.
Ballet, London, 1951.
Photobiography, London, 1951.
Persona Grata, with Kenneth Tynan,
    London, 1953.
The Glass of Fashion, London, 1954.
It Gives Me Great Pleasure, London, 1955.
The Face of The World, London, 1957.
Japanese, London, 1959.
The Wandering Years, London, 1961.
Quail in Aspic, London, 1962.
Images, London, 1963.
Royal Portraits, London, 1963.
Fair Lady, London, 1964.
The Years Between, London, 1965.
The Best of Beaton, London, 1968.
My Bolivian Aunt, London, 1971.
The Happy Years, London, 1972.
The Strenuous Years, London, 1973.
The Magic Image, with Gail Buckland,
    London, 1975.
The Restless Years, London, 1976.
The Parting Years, London, 1978.

Charles Spencer, *Cecil Beaton Stage & Film
    Designs*, London, 1975.
James Danziger, *Beaton*, London, 1980.
Gail Buckland & Peter Quennell, *Cecil
    Beaton War Photographs 1939–45*,
    London, 1981.

The photographs on pages 18, 21, 29, 30, 31, 32 (below), 33, 48 and 54 are reproduced by kind permission of Condé Nast Publications Inc., New York, and that on page 38 by kind permission of Eileen Hose. All other photographs are reproduced by courtesy of Sotheby's.

Index of photographs

Author

Philippe Garner was born in 1949. After graduating from Bedford College, University of London, he joined Sotheby's as a trainee in 1970 and is now a Director, responsible for sales of Decorative Arts from 1880 and for sales of photographic images. He has written extensively on the decorative arts and his publications include the standard biography of Emile Gallé and, most recently, a survey of 'Contemporary Decorative Arts from 1940 to the present day'. He is researching specialized areas of the history of photography with eventual publication in mind, notably the work of 1860s photographer Camille Silvy, the early evolution of photography in Brighton and certain aspects of contemporary commercial photography.

Series Consultant Editors

Romeo Martinez has worked in photographic journalism for over 50 years. Resident in Paris, he is the author of several books on the history of photography and is the editor of the *Bibliothek der Photographie* series. He was responsible for the relaunch on the international market of the magazine *Camera*. From 1957 to 1965, he organized the biennial photographic exhibitions in Venice. Romeo Martinez organized the iconographic department at the Pompidou Centre in Paris. He is a member of the Administration Council and of the Art Commission of the Societé Français de Photographie and a member of the Deutsche Gesellschaft für Photographie.

Bryn Campbell has been active both as a professional photographer and as an editor and writer on photography. He is known to many as the presenter of the BBC TV series *Exploring Photography*. As a photographer, he has worked for a Fleet Street agency, with *The Observer*, and on assignments for *Geo* and *The Observer Magazine*. He has been Assistant Editor of *Practical Photography* and of *Photo News Weekly*, Editor of *Cameras & Equipment*, Deputy Editor of *The British Journal of Photography* and, from 1964 to 1966, Picture Editor of *The Observer*.

In 1974 he was made an Honorary Associate Lecturer in Photographic Arts at the Polytechnic of Central London. The same year he was appointed a Trustee of the Photographers' Gallery, London. He served on the Photography Sub-Committee of the Arts Council and later became a member of the Art Panel. He is a Fellow of the Institute of Incorporated Photographers and a Fellow of the Royal Photographic Society. His book *World Photography* was published in 1981.

First published in 1983 by
William Collins Sons & Co Ltd

London · Glasgow · Sydney
Auckland · Johannesburg

© 1982 Gruppo Editoriale Fabbri S.p.A., Milan

ISBN 0 00 411934 7

Typesetting by Chambers Wallace, London
Printed in Italy